JESUS
ON ETHICS

GUIDANCE FROM THE *WORD OF GOD* AS
RECORDED IN THE ISLAMIC TRADITIONS

**THE
WORLD
FEDERATION**
OF KHOJA SHIA ITHNA-ASHERI MUSLIM COMMUNITIES
www.world-federation.org

Second Edition Published in April 2006 by
The Islamic Education Board of
The World Federation of Khoja Shia Ithna-Asheri Muslim Communities
Registered Charity in the UK No. 282303
Islamic Centre - Wood Lane
Stanmore, Middlesex
United Kingdom
HA7 4LQ
ieb@world-federation.org
www.world-federation.org/ieb

ISBN 1-898449-86-4

Canada Sales and Distribution	**USA Sales and Distribution**
Islamic Humanitarian Service	Darul Tabligh North America
81 Hollinger Crescent · Kitchener, Ontario	786 Summa Avenue · Westbury, NY
Canada, N2K 2Y8	USA, 11590
Tel: 519-576-7111 · Fax: 519-576-8378	Tel: 516-334-2479 · Fax: 516-334-2624
ihs@primus.ca	**www.darultabligh.org**
www.al-haqq.com	**info@darultabligh.org**

Africa Sales & Distribution
Tabligh Sub Committtee · K.S.I. Jama'at Dar es Salaam
P.O. Box 233 · Dar es Salaam, Tanzania
Tel: 255-22-211-5119 Fax: 255-22-211-3107

tabligh@raha.com · www.dartabligh.org

This work contains excerpts from the publication, "Jesus (peace be with him) Through Shi'ite Narrations" selected by Mahdi Muntazir Qa'im and translated Dr. Muḥammad Legenhausen published by Ansariyan Publications of Qum, Iran [ISBN 964-438-609-4]. The selections have been reprinted here with full permission from the copyright holder.

All Qur'ān quotations taken from the English Translation by 'Ali Quli Qara'i.

Table of Contents

In the Name of God, the Most Gracious, the Most Merciful

Introduction

*"I am a hole in a flute by which blows
the breath of Christ, listen to this music."*
Hafiz, the Persian Poet

TODAY WE INCREASINGLY READ that Christianity and Islām 'share' Jesus - that he belongs to both religions. More than ever before, the notion of the 'Abrahamic civilization' where once people spoke of 'Judeo-Christian civilization' includes Islām too. The Qurʾān refers to Prophet Abraham as a monotheist [see Sūrat Āle ʿImrān (3), Verse 67]. According to the Qurʾān, [Sūrat al-Anʿām (6), Verses 85-87] the other prophets sent to mankind, in addition to Prophet Ibrāhīm (Abraham) include (but are not limited to): Ishāq (Isaac), Yaʿqūb (Jacob), Nūh (Noah), Dāwūd (David), Sulaīmān (Solomon), Ayyūb

(Job), Yūsuf (Joseph), Mūsā (Moses), Hārūn (Aaron), Zakariyyā (Zachariah), Ilyās, Ismā'īl (Ishmael), Al-Yash'a (Elisha), Yūnus (Jonah), Lūṭ (Lot), and 'Īsā (Jesus) – God's blessings be upon all of them.

The notion of one God, sharing prominent prophets, and the belief in the afterlife are common between Islām, Judaism, and Christianity. The similarities between Islāmic and Christian thinking about Jesus are equally important: both accept the virgin birth and among the numerous miracles attributed to Jesus in the Glorious Qur'ān are the revival of the dead and the creation of a bird from clay.

There are two main sources in Islām for knowing Jesus. The Qur'ān gives us a history of his life, while the ḥadīth (the traditions of the Prophet Muḥammad (blessings of Allāh be upon him and his family and his Divinely appointed successors) collections establish his revered place in the Muslim understanding. As with previous prophets, Jesus's revelation verified previous prophets' revelations [see Sūrat Āle 'Imrān (3), Verses 49 and 84; Sūrat al-Mā'idah (5),

Verse 46; Sūrat aṣ-Ṣaff (61), Verse 6]. Furthermore, Prophet Muḥammad (blessings of Allāh be upon him and his family) also verified the previous revelations, including the revelation to Jesus (see Sūrat an-Nisā' (4), Verse 47), such that Muslims also believe in the revelation which Jesus received (Sūrat al-Baqarah (2), Verse 136).

Given the commonality of the scriptures and the fact that Muslims and Christians have shared history of some 1,400 years, having lived side by side, one would have thought that they might know each other better. Unfortunately much of that 1,400-year history has been marked by mutual hostility. Whilst there have been periods of mutual respect and peace, the Muslim-Christian relationship has gone through major phases of conflict (the Crusades, colonization and the decline of Muslim civilization). The current phase that began with the tragedy of 9/11, has been a period of searching for real understanding, however, it has been marked by ignorance and stereotyping.

The way forward between the faiths is to begin the process of understanding each other. At this critical point in history where

iii

information technology has shrunk the boundaries of the global village even further, creating friendships and beginning the process of the rediscovery of the meaning of one's faith through dialogue is more important then ever.

One must, however, make the distinction that inter-religious dialogues are not like other dialogues. For example, negotiations between nations, bargaining between labor and management, or any attempt to find middle ground between disputing parties are common forms of dialogue which involve compromise. Compromise often makes a society run better. Labor and management have to compromise or factories don't operate. However, when people of faith have dialogue, they are not attempting any compromise. The primary objective of inter-religious dialogue is not to build one faith for the whole planet, but to share and learn from one another. Inter-religious dialogue can be a process of spiritual growth that can have a transforming effect on those engaged in it, especially when such exchanges are done in the spirit of seeking clarity with humility, kindness, patience, generosity, and trust with a genuine desire to grow in our understanding of the greatness, abundance and mercy of God.

Dr. David Thomas of Selly Oak Colleges, Birmingham, UK who often speaks of the past relations as being "...something of a nightmare, which encumbers Christians and Muslims today with a heavy baggage of memories of war, oppression and conquests" advocates that we go beyond "... the baggage to try to see each other as the other is." He goes even further and states, "...we try to take off our shoes and walk on the holy ground of the other faith ... in order to come back to our own faith as bigger ... more enriched people ready for the encounter to which God calls us."

In the glorious Qur'ān, Jesus is described thus: "O Mary! Verily Allāh gives you the glad tidings of a Word from Him; his name is the Messiah, Jesus son of Mary, prominent in this world and in the Hereafter of those near [to God]." (Sūrat Āle 'Imrān (3), Verse 44) It is in this light that we present this selection of narrations of Prophet Jesus.

The collection in this publication is essentially concerned with ethics and morals. These are as much Christian morals as they are

Islāmic morals. In this day and age of relative morality, the concepts of right and wrong have been muddled by the modern understanding of ethics. The simple yet sublime words of Jesus provide a refreshing insight into unchanging moral values and ethics for all times and for all faiths.

We hope that this publication which offers some reflections on the 'Muslim Jesus' will further enhance understanding between the two great faiths and their inter-religious dialogue. With the portrait of Jesus presented in the Islāmic sources, we demonstrate the reverence Muslims have for Jesus and hope that it will inspire better relations between Muslims and Christians.

Hasnain Walji
Plano, Texas
Muharram 1st 1426 AH
February 10th 2005 CE

Jesus on Ethics – Forty Pieces of Advice from the *Word of God*

The Wealthiest of People

"I entered into the morning among you while my stew has been hunger, my food has been something that grows from the earth for the wild animals and beasts, my lamp has been the moon, my carpet has been the earth, and my pillow has been stone. There is no house for me that may be ruined, no property which may be destroyed, no child who may die, and no wife who may become sad. I enter into the morning while there is nothing for me and enter into the night while there is nothing for me, and I am the wealthiest person among the children of Adam."

The Greatest of Trials

Jesus once asked a person, "What trial remains which has not been visited upon you?" The person replied, "He (God) protected me from a trial which is the greatest of trials - and that is disbelief." Then

Jesus touched the man, and God cured him from his illnesses and beautified his face. He then became a companion of Jesus and worshipped with him.

The Praise of God

It is reported that Jesus passed by a man who was blind, leprous and paralytic, and Jesus heard him giving thanks and saying, "Praise be to God who has protected me from the trials with which He afflicts the majority of mankind."

The Pitfall of Hypocrisy

"I saw a stone upon which was written, 'Turn me over.' I turned it over, and I saw written on it, 'He who does not act according to what he knows will not be blessed in his search for what he does not know and what he knows will come back against him.'"

Kindness to all Creations

Verily, when Jesus, the son of Mary, passed along the shore of a sea,

2

he threw a piece of his bread into the water. Some of the disciples said: "O Spirit of God and His Word! Why did you do this when that was your food?" He said, "I did this in order that some animal amongst the animals of the sea may eat it, and the reward of God for this is great."

Humility to Others

Jesus served a meal to the Apostles and when they had eaten it, he himself washed them. They said, "O Spirit of God! It would have been more proper for us to wash you!" He said, "I did this only that you would do this for those whom you teach."

"O assembly of Apostles! I have a request of you - fulfill it for me." They said, "Your request is fulfilled, O Spirit of God!" Then he stood up and washed their feet. They said, "It would have been more proper for us to have done this, O Spirit of God!" He said, "Verily, it is more fitting for one with knowledge to serve the people. Indeed, I humbled myself only so that you may humble yourselves among the people after me, just as I have humbled myself among you." Then Jesus said, "Wisdom is developed by humility, not by pride, and likewise plants only grow in soft soil, not in stone."

The Trial of the Believer

The disciples complained to Jesus, the son of Mary, about the disrespect of the people for them and their hating them. He said, "Be patient. Likewise, the believers are hated among the people. The example of them is like the example of wheat. How sweet is its taste and how numerous are its enemies."

Providing for Yourself

It is reported that the disciples were the followers of Jesus. Whenever they were hungry they said, "O Spirit of God! We are hungry." Jesus would hit his hands on the ground, whether smooth or hilly, and he would bring out two loaves of bread for each of them. Whenever they were thirsty they said, "O Spirit of God! We are thirsty." Jesus would hit his hands on the ground, and would bring out water, and they drank from it. They asked, "O Spirit of God! Who is better than we are? Whenever we want, we are given food, and whenever we want, water is given to us. We have faith in you and follow you." Jesus said, "Better than you are those who work with their hands and eat from what they earn." After that, the disciples washed clothes by the stream and ate from their wages."

The Best of People

Jesus was asked about the best of people and he said, "One whose speech is the mention of God, whose silence is contemplation, and whose vision is admonition." [That is, he takes a lesson from what he sees.]

The Greatest Action

The disciples asked Jesus, "Indicate to us a work by which we may enter the Garden." He said, "Do not speak at all." They said, "We cannot do that." He said, "Then do not speak except what is good."

A man said to Jesus the son of Mary, "O good teacher, indicate to me a work by which I may enter the Garden." He said to the man, "Beware of God secretly and openly, and do good to your parents."

Jesus, the son of Mary, passed by a group of people who were crying. He asked why they were crying and it was said to him that they were crying for their sins. He said, "You should pray about them and you will be forgiven."

Self-Training

It was said to Jesus, "Who trained you?" He said, "No one trained me. I saw the ugliness of ignorance and so I avoided it."

The Apostles met with Jesus and said to him, "O teacher of the good! Guide us!" He said to them, "Verily Moses the interlocutor of God commanded you not to swear by God, the Blessed and Exalted, falsely, and I command you not to swear by God falsely or in truth."

They said, "O Spirit of God! Guide us more!" He said, "Verily Moses, the prophet of God, commanded you not to commit adultery, and I command you not to talk to yourselves about adultery, let alone to commit adultery. Verily, one who talks to himself about adultery is like the one who sets fire to a room that is decorated, so the smoke damages the decor, even though the room is not burnt."

Having a Good Regard for Others

It is reported that Jesus passed by a carcass with his disciples. The disciples said, "How putrid the smell of this dog is!" Jesus said, "How intense is the whiteness of his teeth!"

Whom to Associate With

The Apostles said to Jesus, "O Spirit of God! With whom should we keep company?" He said, "He, the sight of whom reminds you of God, the speech of whom increases your knowledge, and the works of whom make you desirous of the other world."

Knowing the Prophet

Jesus the son of Mary used to spend some time with the disciples and advise them, and used to say, "He does not know me, who knows not his soul; and he who does not know the soul between his two sides, does not know the soul between my two sides; and he who knows his soul which is between his sides, knows me; and he who knows me, knows He who sent me."

Moral Traits

"He who often becomes upset, his body becomes sick; he whose character is bad, his self becomes his torment; he who often talks, often stumbles; he who often lies, loses his worth; and he who quarrels with men, loses his manliness."

"That which is not loved by you for someone to do to you, do not do that to others; if someone strikes you on the right cheek, turn to him your left cheek also."

"O Children of Israel! Do not be excessive in eating, for those who are excessive in eating are excessive in sleeping; those who are excessive in sleeping are deficient in praying; of those who are deficient in praying, it is written that they are negligent."

"Mind your tongue to reform your heart; be satisfied with your house; beware of pretentiousness and excess; be ashamed before your Lord; cry over your mistakes, and escape from people as you would run from the lion or viper, [for] they were medicine but today, they have become the illness. Then, encounter God when you will."

The Life of the World

"Who would build a house on the waves of the sea? This world is that house, so you should not take it as a dwelling."

"The love of this world and the next cannot be aligned in the heart of a believer, just as water and fire (cannot be contained) in a single vessel."

"When one of you sits in his house he should have clothes on. Verily, God has allotted modesty for you, just as He has allotted your sustenance."

"If you are my lovers and my brothers, you must accustom yourself to the enmity and hatred of the people otherwise you will not be my brothers. I teach you this that you may learn it; I do not teach you so that you may become proud. Verily, you will not achieve that which you desire unless you give up that which you desire, and by enduring patiently that which you detest, and guard your gaze, for it plants lust in the heart, and it is sufficient to tempt an individual. Happy are they who see that which they desire with their eyes, but who commit no disobedience in their hearts. How far is that which is in the past, and how near is that which is to come. Woe to those who have been deluded when what they loathe, approaches them, and what they love abandons them, and there comes that which they were promised. Woe to those whose efforts are for the sake of this world, and whose works are mistaken. How he will be disgraced before his Lord! Moreover, do not speak much for aught, but the remembrance of God. Those who speak much about aught but God harden their hearts, but they do not know it. Do not look at the faults of others over much [the phrase used here indicates spying], but look after the purity of your own selves, for you are enslaved servants. How much water flows in a mountain without its becoming soft? And how much wisdom are you taught without your hearts becoming soft? You are bad servants, and you are not pious servants. You are not nobly free. Indeed, you are like unto the oleander - all who see it wonder at its flower, but when they eat from it, they die. So, peace be unto you."

"This world and the next are rivals. When you satisfy one of them you irritate the other; when you irritate one of them you satisfy the other."

"In truth I say to you, just as one who is sick looks at food and finds no pleasure in it due to the severity of the pain, the masters of this world find no pleasure in worship and do not find the sweetness of it, for what they find is the sweetness of this world. In truth I say to you, just as an animal which is not captured and tamed becomes hardened and its character is changed, so too when hearts are not softened by the remembrance of death and the effort of worship, they become hard and tough. In truth I say to you, if a skin is not torn, it may become a vessel for honey; just as hearts, if they are not torn by desires, or fouled by greed, or hardened by blessings, they may become vessels for wisdom."

"Do not take the world as a master, for it will take you as its servants. Keep your treasure with One who will not squander it. The owners of the treasures of this world fear for its ruin, but he who owns the treasure of God do not fear for its ruin."

Jesus said to the disciples, "Be satisfied with a little of the world, while your religion is safe, likewise the people of this world are satisfied with a little of the religion, while their world is safe; love God by being far from them, and make God satisfied by being angry with them." The disciples said, "O Spirit of God, so with whom should we keep company?" He said, "He, the sight of whom reminds you of God; his speech increases your knowledge and his action makes you desirous of the other world."

Conduct with Others

"O Children of Israel! Do not speak with the ignorant of wisdom, for otherwise you would have done injustice with it (wisdom); and do not keep it (wisdom) from its folk, for otherwise you would have done injustice to them, and do not help the unjust with his injustice, for otherwise your virtue will become void. Affairs are three: the affair whose righteousness is clear to you, so follow it; the affair whose error is clear to you, so avoid it; and the affair about which there are differences, so return it to God, the Almighty and Glorious."

A man said to Jesus, the son of Mary, "O good teacher, indicate to me a work by which I may enter the Garden." Jesus said to him, "Beware of God secretly and openly, and do good to your parents."

Lowering the Gaze

"Beware of looking at what is prohibited, for it is the seed of lust and plant of depravity."

Entering into Paradise

"In truth I say to you, the folds of heaven are empty of the rich; the entering of a camel through the eye of a needle is easier than the entering of a rich man into heaven."

A Prayer of Jesus

Among the supplications narrated from Jesus, the son of Mary, is: "O God! You are the Deity of all who are in heaven and the Deity of all on the earth - there is no Deity in them other than You; and You are the All-wise for all in heaven and the All-wise for all on the earth – there is no All-wise in them other than You; and you are the King of all in heaven and all on the earth – there is no King in them other than You. Your power in heaven is like Your power on the earth. And Your sovereignty in heaven is like Your sovereignty on the earth. I ask you by Your All-generous Name and Your radiant face and Your eternal kingdom, do such and such for me."

It is reported that a man complained to Jesus about his debts. Jesus said to him, "Say: 'O God, Who takes away grief, removes sadness, disposes of sorrow, and answers the prayers of the needy! O Merciful of this world and the other world and the Compassionate of them both! You are Merciful to me and Merciful to all things so, be Merciful to me, with a mercy that will make me needless of the mercy of other than You, and by that mercy, let my debts be paid.'"

Be Critics of Speech

"Take the truth from the folk of falsehood, but do not take the false from the folk of truth. Be critics of speech. How much aberration is adorned by a verse of the Book of God, like the adornment of a copper dirham with silver plating. Looking at it is the same, but those who have vision are aware."

Divine Retribution

It is said that a man accompanied Jesus, the son of Mary, and said that he would go with him. They continued along until they came to a river where they sat and started to eat. They had three loaves of bread from which they ate two of them and one remained. Jesus went to the river, drank some water and returned however upon return, he did not find the third loaf. He asked the man who had taken that loaf and the man replied that he did not know. They continued until they came to a doe followed by two fawns. Jesus beckoned one of the fawns, killed it, roasted it and they ate it. Then Jesus addressed the fawn [that had been eaten,] saying, "Live!" It came to life and went away. Jesus then said to the other man, 'By the God Who has shown you this miracle, who took that loaf of bread?' The man said that he did not know and they continued until they reached a lake. Jesus took the hand of the man and led him over the water. When they reached the other side, Jesus said, 'By the One who has shown you this miracle, who took that loaf of bread?' The man said that he did not know and they continued until they reached a desert and sat down. Jesus gathered some sand or dust and said, "By the permission of God, be gold!" and it became gold. He divided it into three portions and said, "One third is for me, one third for you, and one third for whoever took that loaf of bread." The man said, "Alright, I took that loaf of bread." Jesus said, "All of this gold is yours" and he left him. The man encountered two other men in the desert who wanted to take his gold and kill him. He said, "Let us divide the gold into three portions." They sent one of them to the village to buy food. The one who went said to himself, "Why should I let them have portions of this wealth? I shall put some poison into the food, and kill them." So, the man poisoned the food. The other two people said, "Why should we give a third of this wealth to him? When he comes back, let us kill him, and divide the rest of the wealth between us." When the man returned, they attacked him and killed him, proceeded to eat the (poisoned) food and died. The wealth remained in the desert with the three dead men beside it. Jesus passed them and saw the situation and said to his disciples, "This is the world, so beware of it!"

Life to the Dead

Imam As-Ṣādiq[1] (peace be upon him) was asked, "Did Jesus the son of Mary enliven someone after his death, such that he ate, had a daily living, continued his life for a term and had a child?" He said, "Yes, he had a friend who was a brother in God to him. When Jesus passed by, he would go down to him and Jesus would spend a while with

---

[1] The 6th Divinely appointed successor to the Prophet Muḥammad (blessings of Allāh be upon him and his family) – Ja'far ibne Muḥammad.

him and would then leave with salutations of peace unto him. Once, his mother came out to him [Jesus] and she said to him, 'He died, O Apostle of God!' He said to her, 'Would you like to see him?' She said, 'Yes.' Jesus said to her, 'I will come to you tomorrow to enliven him, with the permission of God.' When the morrow arrived, he came and said to her, 'Accompany me to his grave.' They went to his grave at which point Jesus stopped then called on God. The grave opened and her son came out alive. When his mother saw him and he saw her, they cried. Jesus had mercy on them and said to him, 'Would you like to remain with your mother in the world?' He said, 'O Apostle of God! With eating, a daily living and a term, or without a term, no daily living and no eating?' Jesus said to him, 'But with a daily living, eating and a term. You will live for twenty years, marry and father a child.' He said, 'Yes, in that case.'" [Imām As-Ṣādiq] said, "Jesus returned him to his mother and he lived for twenty years, married and fathered a child."

The Closest Ones to God

Verily, Jesus passed by three people. Their bodies had become thin and their colors had changed. He said, "What has brought you to what I see (this state of yours)?" They said, "Fear of the Fire." He said, "It is the duty of God to give security to those who fear Him." Then he passed from them to three other men. He was surprised to find them even thinner and more changed, and said to them, "What has brought you to what I see?" They said, "Yearning for the Garden." He said, "It is the duty of God to give to him who has hope in Him." Then he passed by three others and was surprised to find them even thinner and their faces were shining like mirrors. He said, "What has brought you to what I see?" They said, "Love of God, the Mighty, and Magnificent." Jesus then said to them, three times, "You are those who are close to God."

Guidance from God revealed to Jesus, the son of Mary

O Jesus! I am your Lord and the Lord of your father.[2] My name is One and I am the One, the Unique in having created everything. All things have been made by Me and all return to Me.

O Jesus! You are the Messiah by My command, and you create from clay what has a shape like a bird by My permission, and you revive the dead by My word. So be one who beseeches Me and one who fears Me, and apart from Me seek no sanctuary except toward Me.

O Jesus! I showed you tenderness through mercy until you became worthy of My friendship because you sought My pleasure. Thus, you were blessed when old and you were blessed when young wherever you were. I bear witness that you are My servant, son of my handmaid. Let Me into your soul as your foremost regard, and make the remembrance of Me the means to your return. Draw near to Me

---

[2] The meaning of his 'father' shall be explained later on in this tradition. (Ed.)

through the supererogatory deeds, and trust in Me that I may suffice for you, and do not trust in any other than Me, so that I abandon you.

O Jesus! Be patient with calamities and be content with the decree. Be in such a way that I will be happy with you, because what pleases Me is obedience without sin.

O Jesus! Enliven the remembrance of Me by your tongue, and let there be love for Me in your heart.

O Jesus! Wake up at the hours of neglecting and give your decisions for My sake with subtle wisdom.

O Jesus! Be one who beseeches and fears Me, and let your heart die in awe of Me.

O Jesus! Be vigilant through the night seeking My pleasure, and thirst through your day for the day when you are in need of Me.

O Jesus! Compete with others by doing good as hard as you can so that you will be well known for good wherever you go.

O Jesus! Judge among My servants though My counsel and establish My justice for I have given you a cure for hearts against satanic disease.

O Jesus! Do not associate with anyone infatuated [with the world].

O Jesus! Indeed I say, no creature believed in Me without becoming humble to Me, and no creature became humble to Me without seeking My requital; so bear witness that such a one is secure from My punishment unless he changes or alters My norm.

O Jesus, son of the Virgin Lady! Weep for yourself with the weeping of one who bade goodbye to his home, deserted this world, and left it to the worldly so that he became one beseeching what is with his God.

O Jesus! In addition, be someone who speaks mildly, who offers greetings vigorously, and who keeps awake while the eyes of the pious sleep. Do this in order to beware of the Day of the Return, severe earthquakes and the terrors of the Resurrection Day when neither household, nor wealth, nor offspring shall profit one.

O Jesus! Adorn your eyes with a touch of sadness when the vain (i.e., foolish) laugh.

O Jesus! Be one of those who humble themselves and are patient, for if you attain that of which the patient have been promised, you are most fortunate.

O Jesus! Day by day abandon this world and taste that which has lost its taste, for truly I tell you: you live to an appointed hour and an appointed day, so pass through this world by what is sufficient for your survival, and be content with coarse food and rough dress. After you have seen what your destiny is to be, know that what you have spent and wasted is recorded.

O Jesus! You are responsible, so be merciful toward the weak, just as I am merciful toward you, and do not be cruel to the orphan.

O Jesus! Weep over yourself in seclusion; let your feet regularly make for the places where prayers are performed, and let Me hear the sweetest melody of the words you say in remembrance of Me. Verily, what I have done for you is good.

O Jesus! I have preserved you for the sins of many nations that I have caused to perish.

O Jesus! Minister to the weak and turn your weary eyes toward the sky and ask your needs from Me, for I am near to you, and do not call upon Me except as one who pleads with Me, and whose concern is a single concern. Then, when you call on Me in this way, I will answer you.

O Jesus! I am not content that the world should be the reward of those who were near you, nor as a chastisement for those you would punish.

O Jesus! You perish and I remain, and your provision is from Me. The term appointed for you is with Me, to Me is your return, and with Me is your reckoning. So ask from Me and do not ask from any other, so that your supplication may be suitable, and I will answer it.

O Jesus! How numerous are people and how few are the number of the patient? The trees are numerous, but those that are good among them are few. Do not be deceived by the beauty of a tree until you taste its fruit.

O Jesus! Do not be deceived by he who rebels against Me by sin. He eats what I have provided for him but he serves another. Then he calls on Me in his sorrow, and I answer him. Then he returns to what he had been doing. Does he rebel against Me or does he seek My wrath? By Me, I have sworn I will take him with a taking from which he cannot be delivered, and from where other than Me he can find no shelter. Where will he escape from My heaven and earth?

O Jesus! Say to the unjust from the children of Israel, do not call upon Me while you are involved in unlawful dealings and there are idols in your houses, for I have resolved that I will respond to them who call upon Me, and My response to their calls will be curses upon them lasting until they disperse.

O Jesus! How long must I wait and hope for good from people while they are heedless and reluctant to return? The words that emit from their mouths do not do not correspond to what is in their hearts, they subject themselves to my loathing, while seeking the love of the believers by [feigning] drawing near to Me.

O Jesus! Let your tongue say the same in secret and in the open, and let your heart and your vision be in accord with that. Turn your heart and your tongue entirely away from the forbidden, and withhold your eyes from anything in which there is no good. How many a beholder has there been whose look planted in their hearts a lust and threw them into the pit of destruction.

O Jesus! Be merciful with great mercy, behave in such a way that you wish others to treat you, increase your remembrance of death and departing from your household, avoid wasting your time, for wasting time corrupts one, and do not be heedless, for he who is heedless of Me is far away from Me. And remember Me by doing righteous acts so that I will remember you.

O Jesus! Turn toward Me after sinning, and remind those who are penitent of Me. Believe in Me and seek nearness to the believers by Me, bid them to call upon Me with you, and beware of the call of the wronged one, for I have resolved to open a gate in the heavens to accept it and to answer him, even if later.

O Jesus! Know that evil ones infect others and the companions of evil

27

cause others to perish, and know those to whom you are near, and choose for yourselves brothers from the believers.

O Jesus! Turn toward Me, for no sin is too great for Me to forgive, as I am the most Merciful of the Merciful. Work for yourself in the period before your death for your heirs may fail to do it for you. Worship Me for a day that is equal to a thousand years of what you reckon in which I repay for the good many times over, and evil deeds will corrupt one who performs them; so prepare the way for yourself throughout the period appointed for you, and compete with others to do whatever is righteous. How many an assembly there have been from which people rose and were then granted sanctuary from the Fire.

O Jesus! Restrain yourself from being involved in this mortal life which comes to an end and follow in the footsteps of those who have lived before you. Call them and speak to them in confidence. Do you feel their presence? Take your advice from them, and know that soon you will join them.

O Jesus! Tell him who rebels against Me by offense and who would compromise [his religion], that he should await My punishment and expect My destruction of him, soon he will be cut off with the destroyed ones. O son of Mary! Blessed are you, that you take your manners from your God, who shows tenderness toward you mercifully; who first bestowed blessings from Himself generously; and He aids you in difficulties. Do not offend, O Jesus! For offenses are not lawful for you. I have made a covenant with you as I made a covenant with those who were before you, and I am a witness of that.

O Jesus! I have honored no creature as I have My religion, and I have not blessed [any creature] with the like of My mercy [for My religion].

O Jesus! Wash your exterior by water and your interior by good deeds, for verily you are returning to Me. Get ready, for that which is coming is near; and let Me hear from you a sad sound.

O Jesus! I have blessed you by grace without pollution, and I sought from you a loan for your soul, then you were stingy, so you will be of those who are destroyed.

O Jesus! Adorn yourself with religion and love of the needy, and walk through the earth modestly. And perform the prayers at any place, for all of them (the lands) are [ritually] clean.

O Jesus! Be prepared for whatever is coming is near, and recite My book while you are [ritually] clean, and make Me hear from you a sad voice.

O Jesus! There is no good in pleasure that does not continue, and in a life for the one who lives it, that fades away.

O son of Mary! If only your eyes could see that which is furnished as a reward for My righteous friends, your heart would melt and your soul would depart longing for it, for there is no abode like that of the other world, where the good live as neighbors, and the cherubim enter it among them, and they are safe from the fear of the day of resurrection. It is an abode in which blessings do not change and are not lost.

O son of Mary! Vie with others for [that abode], for it is the hope of the hopeful, being such a good sight. Blessed are you, O son of Mary, if you work for it, and you are with your fathers, Adam and Abraham in the Garden of bliss, you seek no alternative to it and no change in it. I do this for the God-wary.

O Jesus! Flee toward Me with those who flee from a fire having a dreadful blaze, having chains and shackles into which no gentle wind enters, from which no gloom ever goes, with sectors like those of the dark night, he who is delivered from it will have attained a great achievement, and those who perish will never be delivered from it. It is the abode of tyrants, the wrongdoing oppressors all who are rudely obstinate, and all who are proud boasters.

O Jesus! It is an evil abode for those who rely on it, and evil place to stay, the abode of the oppressors. I warn you of yourself, so, be aware of Me.

O Jesus! Wherever you are, be observant of Me, and bear witness that it is I who created you, that you are My servant, that I formed you, and conveyed you to the earth.

O Jesus! It is not proper for there to be two tongues in one mouth, nor two hearts in one chest, and likewise for minds.

O Jesus! Do not be awake while sinning and do not be aware while wasting time. Wean yourself from destructive lusts and put away every lust that puts you far from Me. Know that to Me, you are a trusted apostle, so be careful of Me. Know that your world will give you back to Me, and I will knowingly take you, so abase yourself when you remember Me. Humble your heart when you remember Me. Be awake during the sleep of the negligent.

O Jesus! This is My advice to you and My admonition to you, so take it from Me and I am the Lord of the worlds.

O Jesus! When My servant is patient for My sake, the reward for his work is from Me, and I am beside him when he calls on Me, and I am sufficient in avenging those who disobey Me. Where will the oppressors go to escape from Me?

O Jesus! Make your speech wholesome, and wherever you are, be both learned and a learner.

O Jesus! Send good deeds to Me, so that they will be remembered by

Me for you, and grasp My advice. Verily, in it there is a cure for hearts.

O Jesus! Do not feel safe when you devise your plans from My plans, and do not forget, when alone in the world, the remembrance of Me.

O Jesus! By returning to Me, take account of yourself, so the reward may be deserved of those who work. They are given their compensation and I am the best of the givers.

O Jesus! You were created by My word. Mary gave birth to you at My command that I sent to her by My spirit, the trusted Gabriel of My angels, until you grew up as one alive and walking; all of this was in My foreknowledge.

O Jesus! Zachariah is in the position of a father to you and as a guardian to your mother. When he went to her in the prayer niche he found with her provisions. John is like you among My creatures. I granted him to his mother when she was old when she did not have the strength for it. By this, I wanted My sovereignty to appear to her and My power to appear in you. The most beloved of you by Me is the most obedient to Me and the most intense of you in fear of Me.

O Jesus! Wake up and do not despair of My mercy and glorify Me with those who glorify Me, and with wholesome speech hallow Me.

O Jesus! How can the servants disbelieve in Me when their forelocks are in My fist and their changes take place on My earth? They are ignorant of My blessings and they are supporters of My enemy, and so the disbelievers are perishing.

O Jesus! Indeed, this world is a foul prison, and the fair seeming in it is, as you see, that over which the tyrants slaughter one another. Beware, the world and all of its blessings will come to an end, and it has but few blessings.

O Jesus! Seek Me when you go to bed, and you will find Me; call upon me while you love Me, and I am the most hearing of the hearers; I answer the callers when they call upon Me.

O Jesus! Fear Me and make My servants fear Me. Happily the sinners may abstain from what they do because of it, so they do not perish unless they knowingly [do it].

O Jesus! Be afraid of Me as you fear predators and death that you meet. I have created all of them, so of Me alone, be afraid.

O Jesus! Verily, Mine is the kingdom and it is in My hand, and I am the King. If you obey Me, I will make you enter My Garden in the vicinity of the righteous.

O Jesus! If I am angry with you, the pleasure of those who are pleased with you will not benefit you, and if I am pleased with you, the anger of those who are angry with you will not harm you.

O Jesus! Remember Me to yourself, and I will remember you to Myself. Remember Me among your people, and I will remember you among a people better than the children of Adam.

O Jesus! Call upon Me with the call of one who is drowning, afflicted, for whom there is none to aid.

O Jesus! Do not swear by Me falsely, so that My Throne shakes with anger. The world is short lived, but is long on hope, and with Me is a realm better than what you gather.

O Jesus! What will you do when I take out for you a book that speaks in truth, while you witness it, of the secrets you have hidden, and the deeds you have done?

O Jesus! Say to the unjust of the Children of Israel: "You wash your faces and soil your hearts. Are you deceived about me, or would you be audacious toward me? For the worldly you use perfumes, but to Me your stomachs are like putrid corpse, as though you were a dead people."

O Jesus! Say to them, "Draw back your hands[3] from illicit gain, stop your ears from listening to curses, and come near to me by your hearts, for your appearance does not appeal to me."

O Jesus! Rejoice in the good deed, for it pleases Me, and weep over the evil deed, for it is a disgrace. That which you do not like to be done unto you, do not do unto others; if one slaps your right cheek, offer him the left one, draw near to Me by your efforts through love, and ignore the ignorant.

---

[3] Literally, "Clip your fingernails from illicit gain."

O Jesus! Be humble toward the doers of good deeds and take part with them in such deeds and be witnesses to them. Say to the unjust of the Children of Israel, "O friends of evil, and those who keep company with it! If you do not comply with the prohibitions, I will transform you into apes and swine."

O Jesus! Say to the unjust of the Children of Israel that wisdom [those who are wise] weeps in fear of Me, while you [Children of Israel] leave laughing. Has there come to you a reprieve, or is there with you a guarantee against My chastisement, or that you will not be subject to My punishment? I swear by Myself, that I will abandon you as an example for those who remain.

Thus I charge you, O son of Mary, that you bring news to the Children of Israel about the Master of the messengers and My beloved, who is named Aḥmad. He has a red camel and a face like the moon, is a shining light, a pure heart, courageous, and venerably modest. Verily, he is a mercy to the worlds, master of the children of

Adam on the day of his meeting Me, the most honored of the foremost[4], the last of the messengers from Me, an Arab, a trustworthy person, one committed to My religion, one patient for My sake, and one who struggles by his hand against the idolaters for the defense of My religion. Order them to affirm him, believe in him, follow him and help him.

Jesus said, "Who is it that I should please? Then, pleasure is for You." God said, "He is Muḥammad the Messenger of God to the people, all of them. In station, he is nearer to Me than they; in intercession, he is more ready than they; blessed be he as a prophet, and blessed be his community if they meet Me on his path. The inhabitants of the earth praise him, and the inhabitants of the heavens ask for his forgiveness. He is the trustworthy, the blessed, the wholesome and salutary and better than others with Me. He will be at the end of time."

---

[4] The foremost are the first to have believed in God.

When he arrives, the spouts of the heavens are loosed, and the earth puts forth its blossoms, so that they see the benediction. I will bless them by that upon which he puts his hand. He has many wives and few children. He is an inhabitant of *Bakkah* (Mecca), the place of the foundations of Abraham.

O Jesus! His religion is upright (*Ḥanifiyyah*), and his *Qiblah* (direction of prayer) is Yemenite[5] and he is of My party, and I am with him, so blessed be he, then blessed be him. The *Kawthar*[6] is for him, and the greatest position in the gardens of Eden. He lives most honored of all who have ever lived, is taken as a martyr, for whom is a fountain greater than the distance from *Bakkah* to the place of the rising of the sun, full of wine untouched, in which there are dishes

---

[5] The portion of the Arabian penninsula including Mecca and Yemen was referred to as Yemenite.

[6] The term *kawthar* has several meanings. Literally it means 'abundant [good]', and in many hadiths it is used in reference to the daughter of the Prophet, Fāṭimah (peace be with her). It is also considered the name of a fountain in heaven.

like the constellations of the sky, and stars like the clods of the earth, in which is every sort of wine and the flavors of every fruit in the Garden. Whoever drinks a drink from it will never thirst.

It is apportioned for him, and I have preferred him by a period of time between you and him. His secrets agree with what is apparent from him, and his words with his actions. He does not command the people, unless he first begins to practice it. His religion is a struggle in hardship and in comfort. The cities will obey him, and the ruler of Rome will humble himself before him following the religion of Abraham. He will mention the Name of God at meals, and bid peace, and he will pray while the people sleep. For him each day there will be five prayers in succession. His call to prayer will be like the call to muster troops. He will open his prayer with *'Allahu Akbar'* (God is the greatest)' and end it with salutations of peace. He will put his feet in line in prayer as the Angels place their feet in line, and his heart and head will be humbled for Me.

Light is in his breast and truth is on his tongue and he is in the right, wherever he is. First an orphan, wandering for a time regarding what He wills for him, his eyes sleep but his heart does not, interceding is only for him, and his community will reach the [Final] Hour[7] and My hand will be above their hands. Whoever breaks [his pledge with the Prophet], breaks [it] against himself, and whoever is loyal to his pledge, I will be loyal to him [awarding to him the Garden]. So command the oppressors of the Children of Israel not to obliterate his books and not to distort his tradition and to offer peace to him. Surely, there is a noble station for him.

O Jesus! Whatever brings you near to Me, I have guided you to it; and all that takes you far from Me, I have prohibited it for you, so, seek what is for your own sake.

O Jesus! Surely this world is sweet, and surely I have employed you in it, so keep aside from you all from which I have warned you, and take from it all that I have given to you in forgiveness.

O Jesus! Look into your deeds with the look of a mistaken sinful

---

[7] This indicates that he will be the final prophet.

41

servant, and do not look into the works of others from the position of Lord. Be without attachment to [this world], and do not long for it, so that it causes you hardship.

O Jesus! Reason about and contemplate and look into the regions of the earth as to what has been the outcome of the oppressors.

O Jesus! All of My attributes are counsel for you, and all of My speech to you is the Truth, and I am the plain Truth. So, in truth I say, "If you disobey me after I informed you, then there is no protector, nor helper for you but Me."

O Jesus! Humble your heart in meekness and look at those who are lower than you and do not look at those who are above you. Know that at the head of every mistake and sin is the love of this world. So, do not love it, for I do not love it either.

O Jesus! Make wholesome your heart for Me and remember Me much in solitude, and know that My pleasure is in your fawning; love Me in an animated and not in a lifeless manner.

O Jesus! Do not make anything My partner, and be wary on account of Me, and do not be deceived by health, so delight in yourself. Surely, this world is like a passing shadow, and what comes from it is like what goes from it. So compete in your struggle for righteousness, and be with truth wherever it is, even if you will be cut or burned by fire. So, do not deny me after knowledge; do not be of the ignorant. A thing is surely with things [of its own sort].

O Jesus! Pour forth tears from your eyes for Me, and humble your heart for Me.

O Jesus! Call on Me for help in hard conditions. I am He who helps those who are upset, and He who answers the destitute, and I am the most Merciful of the merciful."

Jesus, the Son of Mary
in the Noble Qur'ān

"Certainly We gave Moses the Book, and followed him with the apostles; and We gave Jesus, the son of Mary, manifest proofs, and confirmed him with the Holy Spirit. Is it not that whenever an apostle brought you that which was not to your liking, you would act arrogantly; so you would impugn a part [of them], and slay a[nother] part?" (Noble Qur'ān 2:87)

"Say, 'We have faith in God, and that which has been sent down to us, and that which was sent down to Abraham, Ishmael, Isaac, Jacob and the Tribes, and that which Moses and Jesus were given, and that which the prophets were given from their Lord; we make no distinction between any of them, and to Him do we submit.'" (Noble Qur'ān 2:136)

"These are the apostles, some of whom We gave an advantage over others: of them are those to whom God spoke, and some of them He raised in rank, and We gave Jesus, son of Mary, manifest proofs and strengthened him with the Holy Spirit. Had God wished, those who succeeded them would not have fought each other after the manifest proofs had come to them. But they differed. So there were among them those who had faith and there were among them those who were faithless. And had God wished, they would not have fought one another; but God does whatever He desires." (Noble Qur'ān 2:253)

"When the angels said, 'O Mary, God gives you the good news of a Word from Him whose name is Messiah, Jesus, son of Mary, distinguished in the world and the Hereafter, and one of those brought near [to God]. He will speak to people in the cradle and in adulthood, and will be one of the righteous.' She said, 'My Lord, how shall I have a child seeing that no human has ever touched me?' He said, 'So it is that God creates whatever He wishes. When He decides on a matter He just says to it "Be!" and it is. And He will teach him the Book and wisdom, the Torah and the Evangel, and [he will be] an apostle to the Children of Israel, [and he will declare,] 'I have certainly brought you a sign from your Lord: I will create for you out of clay the form of a bird, then I will breathe into it, and it will become a bird by God's leave. And I heal the blind and the leper and I revive the dead by God's leave. And I will tell you what you have eaten and what you have stored in your houses. There is indeed a sign in that for you, should you be faithful. And [I come] to confirm [the truth of] that which is before me of the Torah, and to make lawful for you some of the things that were forbidden you. I have brought you a sign from your Lord; so be wary of God and obey me. Indeed God is my Lord and your Lord; so worship Him. This is a straight path.' And when Jesus sensed their faithlessness, he said, 'Who will be my helpers toward God?' The Disciples said, 'We will be helpers of God. We have faith in God, and bear witness that we are Muslims. Our Lord, we believe in what You have sent down, and we follow the apostle, so write us among the witnesses.'" (Noble Qur'ān 3:45-53)

"When God said, 'O Jesus, I shall take you[r soul], and I shall raise you up toward Myself, and I shall clear you of [the calumnies of] the faithless, and I shall set those who follow you above the faithless until the Day of Resurrection. Then to Me will be your return, whereat I will judge between you concerning that about which you used to differ." (Noble Qur'ān 3:55)

"Indeed the case of Jesus with God is like the case of Adam: He created him from dust, then said to him, 'Be,' and he was." (Noble Qur'ān 3:59)

"Say, 'We have faith in God, and in what has been sent down to us, and what was sent down to Abraham, Ishmael, Isaac, Jacob and the Tribes, and that which Moses and Jesus were given, and the prophets, from their Lord. We make no distinction between any of them, and to Him do we submit.'" (Noble Qur'ān 3:84)

"Then because of their breaking their covenant, their defiance of God's signs, their killing of the prophets unjustly and for their saying, 'Our hearts are covered over.' Rather God has set a seal on them for their unfaith, so they do not have faith except a few. And for their faithlessness, and their uttering a monstrous calumny against Mary, and for their saying, 'We killed the Messiah, Jesus son of Mary, the apostle of God' — though they did not kill him nor did they crucify him, but so it was made to appear to them. Indeed those who differ concerning him are surely in doubt about him: they do not have any knowledge of that beyond following conjectures, and certainly they did not kill him. Rather God raised him up toward Himself, and God is all-mighty, all-wise. There is none among the People of the Book but will surely believe in him before his death; and on the Day of Resurrection he will be a witness against them." (Noble Qur'ān 4:155-159)

49

"We have indeed revealed to you as We revealed to Noah and the prophets after him, and [as] We revealed to Abraham and Ishmael, Isaac, Jacob, and the Tribes, Jesus and Job, Jonah, Aaron, and Solomon — and We gave David the Psalms." (Noble Qur'ān 4:163)

"O People of the Book! Do not exceed the bounds in your religion, and do not attribute anything to God except the truth. The Messiah, Jesus son of Mary, was only an apostle of God, and His Word that He cast toward Mary and a spirit from Him. So have faith in God and His apostles, and do not say, '[God is] a trinity.' Relinquish [such a creed]! That is better for you. God is but the One God. He is far too immaculate to have any son. To Him belongs whatever is in the heavens and whatever is on the earth, and God suffices as trustee. The Messiah would never disdain being a servant of God, nor would the angels brought near [to Him]. And whoever disdains His worship and is arrogant, He will gather them all toward Him." (Noble Qur'ān 4:171-172)

"They are certainly faithless who say, 'God is the Messiah, son of Mary.' Say, 'Who can avail anything against God should He wish to destroy the Messiah, son of Mary, and his mother, and everyone upon the earth?' To God belongs the kingdom of the heavens and the earth, and whatever is between them. He creates whatever He wishes, and God has power over all things." (Noble Qur'ān 5:17)

"And We followed them with Jesus son of Mary, to confirm that which was before him of the Torah, and We gave him the Evangel containing guidance and light, confirming what was before it of the Torah, and as guidance and advice for the Godwary." (Noble Qur'ān 5:46)

"They are certainly faithless who say, 'God is the Messiah, son of Mary.' But the Messiah had said, 'O Children of Israel! Worship God, my Lord and your Lord. Indeed whoever ascribes partners to God, God shall forbid him [entry into] Paradise, and his refuge shall be the Fire, and the wrongdoers will not have any helpers.' They are certainly faithless who say, 'God is the third [person] of a trinity,' while there is no god except the One God. If they do not relinquish what they say, there shall befall the faithless among them a painful punishment." (Noble Qur'ān 5:72-73)

"The Messiah, son of Mary, is but an apostle. Certainly [other] apostles have passed before him, and his mother was a truthful one. Both of them would eat food. Look how We clarify the signs for them, and yet, look, how they go astray!" (Noble Qur'ān 5:75)

"When God will say, O Jesus son of Mary, remember My blessing upon you and upon your mother, when I strengthened you with the Holy Spirit, so you would speak to the people in the cradle and in adulthood, and when I taught you the Book and wisdom, the Torah and the Evangel, and when you would create from clay the form of a bird, with My leave, and you would breathe into it and it would become a bird, with My leave; and you would heal the blind and the leper, with My leave, and you would raise the dead, with My leave;

52

and when I held off [the evil of] the Children of Israel from you when you brought them manifest proofs, whereat the faithless among them said, 'This is nothing but plain magic.' And when I inspired the Disciples, [saying], 'Have faith in Me and My apostle,' they said, 'We have faith. Bear witness that we are Muslims.' When the Disciples said, 'O Jesus son of Mary! Can your Lord send down to us a table from the sky?' Said he, 'Be wary of God, should you be faithful.' They said, 'We desire to eat from it, and our hearts will be at rest: we shall know that you have told us the truth, and we shall be among the witnesses to it.' Said Jesus son of Mary, 'O God! Our Lord! Send down to us a table from the sky, to be a festival for us, for the first ones and the last ones among us and as a sign from You, and provide for us; for You are the best of providers.' God said, 'I will indeed send it down to you. But should any of you disbelieves after this, I will indeed punish him with a punishment such as I do not punish anyone in all creation.' And when God will say, 'O Jesus son of Mary! Were it you who said to the people, "Take me and my mother for gods besides God"?' He will say, 'Immaculate are You! It does not behoove me to say what I have no right to [say]. Had I said it, You

53

would certainly have known it: You know whatever is in my self, and I do not know what is in Your Self. Indeed You are knower of all that is Unseen. I did not say to them [anything] except what You had commanded me [to say]: "Worship God, my Lord and your Lord." And I was a witness to them so long as I was among them. But when You had taken me away, You Yourself were watchful over them, and You are witness to all things. If You punish them, they are indeed Your creatures; but if You forgive them, You are indeed the All-mighty, the All-wise.' God will say, 'This day truthfulness shall benefit the truthful. For them there will be gardens with streams running in them, to remain in them forever. God is pleased with them and they are pleased with Him. That is the great success.'" (Noble Qur'ān 5:110-119)

"[This is] an account of your Lord's mercy on His servant, Zechariah, when he called out to his Lord with a secret cry. He said, 'My Lord! Indeed my bones have become feeble, and my head has turned white with age, yet never have I, my Lord, been disappointed in supplicating You! Indeed I fear my kinsmen, after me, and my wife is barren. So grant me from Yourself an heir who may inherit from me and inherit from the House of Jacob, and make him, my Lord, pleasing [to You]!' 'O Zechariah! Indeed We give you the good news of a son, whose name is "John." Never before have We made anyone his namesake.' He said, 'My Lord! How shall I have a son, when my wife is barren, and I am already advanced in age?' He said, 'So shall it be. Your Lord has said, "It is simple for Me." Certainly I created you before when you were nothing.' He said, 'My Lord! Appoint a sign for me.' He said, 'Your sign is that you will not speak to the people for three complete nights.' So he emerged before his people from the Temple, and signaled to them that they should glorify [God] morning and evening. 'O John!' [We said,] 'Hold on with power to the Book!' And We gave him judgement while still a child, and a compassion and purity from Us. He was Godwary, and good to his parents, and was not self-willed or disobedient. Peace be to him, the day he was born, and the day he dies, and the day he is raised alive! And mention in the Book Mary, when she withdrew from her family to an easterly place. Thus did she seclude herself from them, uwhereupon We sent to her Our Spirit and he became incarnate for her as a well-proportioned human. She said, 'I seek the protection of the All-beneficent from you, should you be Godwary!' He said, 'I am only a messenger of your Lord that I may give you a pure son.' She said, 'How shall I have a child seeing that no human being has ever touched me, nor have I been unchaste?' He said, 'So shall it be. Your Lord says, "It is simple for Me." And so that We may make him a sign for mankind and a mercy from Us, and it is a matter [already] decided.' Thus she conceived him, then withdrew with him to a distant place. The birth pangs brought her to the trunk of a date palm. She said, 'I wish I had died before this and become a forgotten thing, beyond recall.' Thereupon he called her from below her [saying,] 'Do not grieve! Your Lord has made a spring to flow at your feet. Shake the trunk of the palm tree, freshly picked dates will drop upon you. Eat, drink, and be comforted. Then if you see any human, say, "Indeed I have vowed a fast to the All-beneficent, so I will not speak to any human today."' Then carrying him she brought him to her people. They said, 'O Mary, you have certainly come up with an odd thing! O sister of Aaron['s lineage]! Your father was not an evil man, nor was your mother unchaste.' Thereat she pointed to him. They said, 'How can we speak to one who is yet a baby in the cradle?' He said, 'Indeed I am a servant of God! He has given me the Book and made me a prophet. He has made me blessed, wherever I may be, and He has enjoined me to [maintain] the prayer and to [pay] the zakat as long as I live, and to be good to my mother, and He has not made me self-willed and wretched. Peace is to me the day I was born, and the day I die, and the day I am raised alive.' That is Jesus, son of Mary, a Word of the Real concerning whom they are in doubt. It is not for God to take a son. Immaculate is He! When He decides on a matter, He just says to it, 'Be!' and it is." (Noble Qur'ān 19:2-35)

"When the Son of Mary was cited as an example, behold, your people raise an outcry. They say, 'Are our gods better or he?' They only cite him to you for the sake of contention. Rather they are a contentious lot. He was just a servant whom We had blessed and made an exemplar for the Children of Israel. Had We wished We would have set in your stead angels to be [your] successors on the earth. Indeed he is a portent of the Hour; so do not doubt it and follow Me. This is a straight path. Do not let Satan bar you [from the way of God]. Indeed he is your manifest enemy. When Jesus brought the manifest proofs, he said, 'I have certainly brought you wisdom, and [I have come] to make clear to you some of the things that you differ about. So be wary of God and obey me.' Indeed God is my Lord and your Lord; so worship Him. This is a straight path.' But the factions differed among themselves. So woe to the wrongdoers for the punishment of a painful day. Do they await anything but that the Hour should overtake them suddenly, while they are unaware?" (Noble Qur'ān 43:57-66)

"And when Jesus son of Mary said, 'O Children of Israel! Indeed I am the apostle of God to you, to confirm what is before me of the Torah, and to give the good news of an apostle who will come after me, whose name is Ahmad.' Yet when he brought them manifest proofs, they said, 'This is plain magic.'" (Noble Qur'ān 61:6)

"O you who have faith! Be God's helpers, just as Jesus son of Mary said to the disciples, 'Who will be my helpers for God's sake?' The Disciples said, 'We will be God's helpers!' So a group of the Children of Israel believed, and a group disbelieved. Then We strengthened the faithful against their enemies, and they became the dominant ones." (Noble Qur'ān 61:14)

Frequently Asked Questions about Jesus

1. Do Muslims believe that Jesus was a Messenger of God?

YES! Belief in all of the Prophets and Messengers of God, which according to Islamic sources number 124,000, is a fundamental article of faith in Islam. Thus, believing in Prophets Adam, Noah, Abraham, Ishmael, Isaac, David, Jacob, Jesus, Moses, and Muhammad (peace and blessings be upon all of them) is a prerequisite for anyone wanting to call him or herself a Muslim. A person claiming to be a Muslim who, for instance, denies the Messengership of Jesus, is not considered a Muslim.

In regards to the status of Jesus as a Messenger, the Qur'ān says: *"Say, 'We have faith in God, and that which has been sent down to us, and that which was sent down to Abraham, Ishmael, Isaac, Jacob and the Tribes, and that which Moses and Jesus were given, and that which the prophets were given from their Lord; we make no distinction between any of them, and to Him do we submit.'"* (Noble Qur'ān 2:136)

2. Do Muslims believe Jesus was born of a Virgin Mother?

YES! Just like the Christians, Muslims also believe Mary, *Maria* in Spanish, *Mariam* in Hebrew, or *Maryam* as she is called in 'Arabic, was a chaste, virgin woman, who miraculously conceived and gave birth to Jesus.

Excerpts of her blessed life are retold in the Qur'ān in chapter 19 (Chapter Mary), a portion of which reads: *"And mention in the Book, Mary, when she withdrew from her family to an easterly place. Thus did she seclude herself from them, whereupon, We sent to her Our Spirit and he became incarnate for her as a well-proportioned human. She said, 'I seek the protection of the All-beneficent from you, should you be Godwary!' He said, 'I am only a messenger of your Lord that I may give you a pure son.' She said, 'How shall I have a child seeing that no human being has ever touched me, nor have I been unchaste?' He said, 'So shall it be. Your Lord says, "It is simple for Me." And so that We may make him a sign for mankind and a mercy from Us, and it is a matter [already] decided.'"* (Noble Qur'ān 19:16-21)

3. Do Muslims believe that Jesus had a miraculous birth?

YES! In quoting the words of Mary, God states in the Noble Qur'ān that: *"When the angels said, 'O Mary, God gives you the good news of a Word from Him whose name is Messiah, Jesus, son of Mary, distinguished in the world and the Hereafter, and one of those brought near [to God]. He will speak to people in the cradle and in adulthood, and will be one of the righteous.' She said, 'My Lord, how shall I have a child seeing that no human has ever touched me?' He said, 'So it is that God creates whatever He wishes. When He decides on a matter He just says to it "Be!" and it is. And He will teach him the Book and wisdom, the Torah and the Evangel, and [he will be] an apostle to the Children of Israel..."* (Noble Qur'ān 3:45-49)

It should also be noted about his creation and birth that the Qur'ān informs its readers that: *"Indeed the case of Jesus with God is like the case of Adam: He created him from dust, then said to him, 'Be,' and he was."* (Noble Qur'ān 3:59)

4. Do Muslims believe Jesus spoke in the cradle?

YES! One of the miracles of Jesus was that he spoke while an infant in defense of his mother.

The Noble Qur'ān states: *"Then if you see any human, say, "Indeed I have vowed a fast to the All-beneficent, so I will not speak to any human today."" Then carrying him she brought him to her people. They said, 'O Mary, you have certainly come up with an odd thing! O sister of Aaron['s lineage]! Your father was not an evil man, nor was your mother unchaste.' Thereat she pointed to him. They said, 'How can we speak to one who is yet a baby in the cradle?' He said, 'Indeed I am a servant of God! He has given me the Book and made me a prophet. He has made me blessed, wherever I may be, and He has enjoined me to [maintain] the prayer and to [pay] the charity as long as I live, and to be good to my mother, and He has not made me self-willed and wretched. Peace is to me the day I was born, and the day I die, and the day I am raised alive.' That is Jesus, son of Mary, a Word of the Real concerning whom they are in doubt."* (Noble Qur'ān, 19:27-34)

5. Do Muslims believe he performed miracles?

YES! Muslims, like Christians believe Jesus performed miracles. However Muslims believe that these were performed by the will and permission of God, Who has power and control over all things.

The Noble Qur'ān tells us: *"When God will say, O Jesus son of Mary, remember My blessing upon you and upon your mother ... and when you would create from clay the form of a bird, with My leave, and you would breathe into it and it would become a bird, with My leave; and you would heal the blind and the leper, with My leave, and you would raise the dead, with My leave; and when I held off [the evil of] the Children of Israel from you when you brought them manifest proofs, whereat the faithless among them said, 'This is nothing but plain magic.'"* (Noble Qur'ān, 5:110-110)

6. Do Muslims believe in the Trinity?

NO! Muslims believe in the Absolute Oneness of God – the Supreme Being free of human limitations, needs and wants. He has no partners in His Divinity. He is the Creator of everything and is completely separate from His creation.

God says in the Noble Qur'ān regarding the Trinity: *"O People of the Book! Do not exceed the bounds in your religion, and do not attribute anything to God except the truth. The Messiah, Jesus son of Mary, was only an apostle of God, and His Word that He cast toward Mary and a spirit from Him. So have faith in God and His apostles, and do not say, '[God is] a trinity.' Relinquish [such a creed]! That is better for you. God is but the One God. He is far too immaculate to have any son. To Him belongs whatever is in the heavens and whatever is on the earth, and God suffices as trustee. The Messiah would never disdain being a servant of God, nor would the angels brought near [to Him]. And whoever disdains His worship and is arrogant, He will gather them all toward Him."* (Noble Qur'ān 4:171-172)

7. Do Muslims believe that Jesus was the son of God?

NO! The Noble Qur'ān informs us: *"Say, 'He is God, the God is the All-embracing. He neither begat, nor was begotten, nor has He any equal.'"* (Noble Qur'ān 112:1-4)

The Qur'ān also states that, *"Jesus, son of Mary, a Word of the Real concerning whom they are in doubt. It is not for God to take a son. Immaculate is He! When He decides on a matter, He just says to it, 'Be!' and it is."* (Noble Qur'ān 19:34-35)

8. Do Muslims believe Jesus was killed on the cross then resurrected?

NO! The Muslims categorically reject the notion that this great Prophet was crucified or killed in any form.

The Noble Qur'ān tells us, *"Then because of their breaking their covenant, their defiance of God's signs, their killing of the prophets unjustly and for their saying, 'Our hearts are covered over.' Rather God has set a seal on them for their unfaith, so they do not have faith except a few. And for their faithlessness, and their uttering a monstrous calumny against Mary, and for their saying, 'We killed the Messiah, Jesus son of Mary, the apostle of God' — though they did not kill him nor did they crucify him, but so it was made to appear to them. Indeed those who differ concerning him are surely in doubt about him: they do not have any knowledge of that beyond following conjectures, and certainly they did not kill him. Rather*

God raised him up toward Himself, and God is all-mighty, all-wise. There is none among the People of the Book but will surely believe in him before his death; and on the Day of Resurrection he will be a witness against them. "(Noble Qur'ān 4:155-159)

We also read, *"Rather, God raised him up to Himself, and God is all-mighty, all-wise."* (Noble Qur'ān 4:158)

Jesus at a glance in the faiths of Christianity, Islam and Judaism

Concept	Christianity	Islam	Judaism
1. Miraculous birth	Yes	Yes	No
2. Miracles	Yes	Yes	No
3. Status	Messiah and Son of God.	Prophet and Messenger.	No
4. Revelation	Gospels written by different authors.	Injīl (Evangel) revealed by God to Jesus.	No
5. Death and After	Crucified for the redemption of sins and resurrected after three days.	Never crucified; taken to the Heavens by God.	Crucified and died.

Sources for this Work[8]

Biḥārul Anwār is a collection of aḥādīth (sayings of the Propht Muḥammad and his twelve appointed sucessors) in ʿArabic compiled by Mawlā Muḥammad Bāqir ibn Muḥmmad Taqī, known as Majlisī the Second, or simply ʿAllāmah Majlisī (d. 1110 AH/1689 CE). He is one of the most prolific Shīʿī writers, and was Shaykh al-Islām during the Safavid period. He authored thirteen books in ʿArabic and fifty-three in Farsi. His largest and most important work is *Biḥārul Anwār al-Jāmiʿah li-Durar Akhbār al-Aʾimmah al-Aṭhār.* This is the most comprehensive of all collections of Shīʿī aḥādīth, and it includes almost all aḥādīth attributed to the Prophet through Shīʿī chains of transmission, almost all of the aḥādīth Qudsī (narrations of the words of God revealed to the Prophet not included in the Qurʾān), and other narrations attributed to the Imams (peace be upon all of them).

---

[8] This detailed look at the sources of this work has been taken from the original publication , *Jesus Through Shiʿite Narrations*, by Muḥammad Legenhausen.

One of the features of this work is that 'Allāmah Majlisī went to great pains to separate his own views from the transmission of the aḥādīth. It took him thirty-six years to compile the work, from 1070 AH to 1106 AH (1649 CE to 1685 CE), with the cooperation of other scholars of the day and students.

In the first volume, he identifies his sources, and later in the same volume he evaluates their reliability. His sources include close to four hundred titles, among which are sixteen works of Shaykh Ṣadūq, sixteen works of Shaykh Ṭūsī, eighteen works of Shaykh Mufīd, twelve works of Sayyid Murtaḍā, twelve works of Shahīd Awwal, twenty-one works of Sayyid ibn Ṭāwūs, twenty-three works of 'Allāmah Ḥillī and twelve works of Shahīd Thānī. He also made use of ninety works by Sunnī authors for correcting the words of the narrations or determining their meanings, and he mentions each of these sources by name in his introduction.

There are three extant editions that have been published of *Biḥārul Anwār*. One is a lithograph print in twenty-five volumes, known as the old edition. The second is that of Dar al-Kutub al-Islāmiyyah,

Tehran, Bazār Sulaīmānī, in one hundred ten volumes (no date), known as the new edition. In the Tehran edition, volumes 54, 55 and 56 contain a table of contents. The third edition is really just a reprint of the Tehran edition published by Mu'assasah al-Wafā' of Beirut. In the Beirut edition, the contents have been moved to volumes 108, 109 and 110, and a volume 0 was added in which there is an introduction to the author and the authors of his sources.[9] We have used the new edition published in Tehran.

Tuḥaf al-ʿUqūl fī Mā Jā'a min al-Ḥikam wa al-Mawāʿiḍ ʿan Āl-Rasūl by Abī Muḥammad Ḥasan ibn ʿAlī ibn Ḥusayn ibn Shuʿbah Ḥarrānī Ḥalabī is one of the most well known collections of Shīʿī narrations. The author was a contemporary of Shaykh Ṣadūq and died in 381 AH (960 CE). Shaykh Mufīd reports narrations from him, and he, in turn, reports traditions from Shaykh Abū ʿAlī Muḥammad ibn Hammām,

---

[9] This infomation is given in the article, *Biḥārul Anwār*, by Bahāʿ al-Dīn Khoramshāhī in Dayirah al-Maʿārif Tashshayyuʿ, Volume 3, (Tehran: Mu'assasah Dayirah al-Maʿārif Tashshayyuʿ, 1371 AH /1992 CE), Page 91-98.

who died in 336 AH (1005 CE). The book contains narrations from the Prophet followed by narrations of the first eleven Imams (peace be upon all of them). After this, there are four more parts to the book: (1) the whispered counsel (munājāt) of God to Moses (peace be upon him); (2) the whispered counsel of God to Jesus (peace be upon him); (3) the advice of the Messiah (peace be upon him) in the gospel and other places; and (4) advice of Mufaḍḍal ibn ʿUmar, one of the companions of Imam Ṣādiq (peace be upon him), to the Shīʿa. In the introduction to this work, Ibn Shuʿbah writes:

"I did not mention the chains of transmission in order to reduce the volume of the book and keep it short. Most of the narrations in this book are ones I have heard. Most of them pertain to manners and wisdom which testify to their own validity and the correctness of their attribution."

Scholars in this field consider the work to be reliable and refer to it in support of their opinions about aḥādīth and fiqh. The book was first published in 1303 AH (1883 CE) in Iran, and later in Iraq, Lebanon and Iran.[10] The edition we have used is that of Qom, Mu'assasah al-Nashr al-Islāmī, 1416 AH (1996 ce).

The narrations we have translated from *Tuḥaf al-ʿUqūl* are given without mention of a chain of transmission, although there is an indication in this work that they are reported by Imām Mūsā ibn Jaʿfar al-Kāẓim (peace be upon him).[11] Part of the narration may also be found in al-Kāfī, Volume 2, Page 319, attributed to Imām Ṣādiq (peace be upon him).

Al-Kāfī is one of the four most authoritative sources of Shīʿī narrations. It was compiled by Muḥammad ibn Yaʿqūb ibn Isḥāq al-Kulaynī al-Rāzī (d. 328 AH) and contains six thousand narrations divided into thirty-four sections. It took twenty years to write

---

[10] See the article, *Tuḥaf al-ʿUqūl*, by Sayyid Mahdī Ḥāʾirī in Dayirah al-Maʿārif Tashshayyuʿ, Volume 4, (Tehran: Mu'assasah Dayirah al-Maʿārif Tashshayyuʿ, 1373 AH /1994 CE), Page 169.
[11] *Tuḥaf al-ʿUqūl*, Page 392

during the minor occultation of the twelfth Imām (peace be upon him). It has been published in eight volumes in Tehran by Dār al-Kutub al-Islāmiyyah. We have used the 1362 AH /1983 CE edition. The whispered counsel of God to Jesus (peace be upon him), taken from *al-Kāfī*, Volume 8, Pages 131-141, may also be found in *Tuḥaf al-ʿUqūl*, Page 496, without mention of the name of the Imām from whom it was narrated, and in *Al-Amālī* of Shaykh Ṣadūq it is narrated from Imām Ṣādiq (peace be upon him).

Another of the "four books" of Shīʿī narrations containing reports about Jesus (peace be upon him) is *Tahdhīb al-Aḥkām* by Shaykh al-Ṭāʾifah Abī Jaʿfar Muḥammad ibn al-Ḥasan ibn ʿAlī al-Ṭūsī (d. 460 AH/1039 CE). There are said to have been four hundred small books of Shīʿī narrations extant during the author's lifetime, known as Uṣūl al-Arbaʿah Miʾah, and the author claims to have compiled this collection from these. This book is a commentary on *Al-Muqniʿah* of Shaykh Mufīd, a work of jurisprudence containing references to aḥādīth. The edition of the *Tahdhīb al-Aḥkām* we have used is that of Tehran Dār al-Kutub al-Islāmiyyah (no date).

74

Mustadrak al-Wasā'il wa Mustanbaṭ al-Masā'il by Ḥājj Mīrzā Ḥusayn Nūrī al-Ṭabarsī ibn Muḥammad Taqī (d. 1320 AH/1899 CE) contains more than twenty-three thousand narrations and has been published in Qom by Mu'assasah Āl al-Bayt li Iḥyā' al-Turāth, first edition published in 1408 AH (1988 CE). This is considered one of the four most important collections of Shī'ī ḥadīth of the modern period, that is, after the eleventh/seventeenth century. The others being *Al-Wāfī* by Faiḍ Kāshanī, *Biḥārul Anwār* by 'Allāmah Majlisī and *Wasā'il al-Shī'ah* by Shaykh Ḥurr al-'Āmilī. It was written in order to complete the narrations not included in the *Wasā'il al-Shī'ah*.

"[Jesus, son of Mary, said to the Israelites]: '...and I give you the glad tidings of the coming of a Messenger who will come after me named Aḥmad [Muḥammad].'"

Noble Qur'ān Sūratul Ṣaff (61), Verse 6